Columbia Space Shuttle Explosion and Space Exploration

A MODERN PERSPECTIVES BOOK

Tamra B. Orr

Published in the United States of America by Cherry Lake Publishing
Ann Arbor, Michigan
www.cherrylakepublishing.com

Content Adviser: Satta Sarmah Hightower, Writer & Editor, Talented Tenth Media, Boston, MA
Reading Adviser: Marla Conn MS, Ed., Literacy specialist, Read-Ability, Inc.

Photo Credits: NASA/Kennedy Space Center, cover, 1; ©michaeljung / Shutterstock.com, 4; ©
Sergey Kohl / Shutterstock.com, 5; NASA, 7, 12, 19, 23, 29; NASA/Bill Ingalls, 9; NASA/James
Blair, 10; NASA/Kim Shiflett, 11, 30; © Black-Photogaphy / Shutterstock.com, 14; © Feel good
studio / Shutterstock.com, 15; NASA/Elizabeth Landau, 21; © nd3000 / Shutterstock.com, 17; ©
bikeriderlondon / Shutterstock.com, 22; © africa924 / Shutterstock.com, 25

Graphic Element Credits: ©RoyStudioEU/Shutterstock.com, back cover, front cover, multiple
interior pages; ©queezz/Shutterstock.com, back cover, front cover, multiple interior pages

Library of Congress Cataloging-in-Publication Data
Names: Orr, Tamra, author.
Title: Columbia Space Shuttle explosion and space exploration / Tamra B. Orr.
Description: Ann Arbor : Cherry Lake Publishing, 2017. | Series: Modern perspectives | Audience:
    Grades 4 to 6. | Includes bibliographical references and index.
Identifiers: LCCN 2016058626| ISBN 9781634728614 (hardcover) | ISBN 9781534100398
    (paperback) | ISBN 9781634729505 (PDF) | ISBN 9781534101289 (hosted ebook)
Subjects: LCSH: Columbia (Spacecraft)—Juvenile literature. | Columbia (Spacecraft)—
    Accidents—Juvenile literature. | Space shuttles—Accidents—Juvenile literature. |
    Explosions—History—21st century—Juvenile literature.
Classification: LCC TL867 .O745 2017 | DDC 363.12/4—dc23
LC record available at https://lccn.loc.gov/2016058626

Cherry Lake Publishing would like to acknowledge the work of
The Partnership for 21st Century Skills. Please visit *www.p21.org*
for more information.

Printed in the United States of America
Corporate Graphics

Table of Contents

In this book, you will read three different perspectives about the *Columbia* space shuttle explosion, which happened on February 1, 2003. While these characters are fictionalized, each perspective is based on real things that happened to real people during and after the explosion. As you'll see, the same event can look different depending on one's point of view.

Chapter 1

Rosario Torres

WRDY News Reporter

I took a deep breath, then another one. I stood up straighter and squared my shoulders. I was a professional, and people all over the viewing area were waiting for me to tell them what was happening. I was a reporter, and I had to be able to report, regardless of how upset I might be feeling.

"Okay, Rosie," shouted Raj, my cameraman. "Ready? You're on in 3, 2, 1 . . ." I watched his fingers count down the last seconds. As he said "1," I saw the camera focus tightly on my face.

"This is Rosario Torres for WRDY News, reporting live from the Kennedy Space Center," I began. I was relieved that my voice sounded

▲ *Television and print journalists must respond quickly to national events.*

much stronger than I felt inside. "Just moments ago, the space shuttle *Columbia* exploded during **reentry**." I paused for a moment to steady my voice.

"At the time, it was flying at 18 times the speed of sound and was about 201,000 feet (61,265 meters) above Dallas, Texas," I continued. "According to **NASA** reports, the explosion was caused by a problem originally observed during the shuttle's **launch** 16 days ago. Apparently a laptop-sized piece of foam fell off of the shuttle's external fuel tank 82 seconds after **liftoff**. The foam struck the shuttle's left wing and punched a hole, as well as cracking some of the wing's heat-resistant tiles. During reentry, superheated air entered through the

Second Source

▶ Find a video that shows what happened that day. How does the information in that source compare to the information in this source?

▲ *The Space Shuttle program operated 135 missions between 1981 and 2011.*

Think About It

▶ Read the paragraph about what happened to the *Columbia*. In your own words, describe what happened to the shuttle.

hole created by the foam, leading to the failure of the wing and, ultimately, the shuttle."

Raj gave me a thumbs-up and signaled me to keep talking. I was glad I had gotten so many details from Allen Gregory, one of the NASA representatives speaking to the press. "Although NASA was aware of what happened during the launch, they did not realize that the foam had damaged the wing so severely," I explained. I could imagine how everyone inside NASA was in shock and trying quickly to figure out what they had missed.

"The seven-member crew of Mission STS-107 was returning from a research mission and sadly, none of the astronauts survived the explosion," I said, trying to keep my voice from shaking. I knew that the news channels would be filled with the life stories and photos of

▲ *NASA employs people to work directly with the press to be sure the public is informed.*

▲ The Columbia *crew trained for many hours before their mission.*

the crew for weeks to come. I felt such sadness for the team's families and friends. "The crew had spent over two weeks doing science experiments around the clock," I added. "Over 80 experiments were finished, with the crew working 24 hours a day in two shifts."

Raj's hand went up in the air, warning me that I had a minute of airtime left before the station would return to the main news desk. "Search-and-rescue teams have been sent to east Texas and west Louisiana to see what can be found in the wreckage," I said. "Hopefully they will find something that will help further explain how this international tragedy happened and figure out how to prevent it from happening again. This is Rosario Torres for WRDY."

▲ *NASA held many press conferences in the wake of the* Columbia *disaster. Topics ranged from the* Columbia*'s timeline to plans for the memorials for the* Columbia *crew.*

▲ *The crew members of the* Columbia *mission were between the ages of 41 and 48.*

The camera light went out, and Raj smiled at me. "Good job, Rosie," he said. He knew I had been struggling to stay calm and unemotional during the report. "I've been a cameraman for a dozen different reporters over the years," he confided to me. "Believe me, it is the ones who are shaken by what they are reporting whom people end up trusting the most. Emotions show that you care, and that is one of the most important parts of the job."

I smiled. I did care—and I was sure I would remember Raj's advice and today's tragic loss of life for the rest of my career.

Columbia Crew Members

Name	Crew Position
Rick Husband	Commander
Michael Anderson	**Payload** commander
David Brown	Mission specialist
Kalpana Chawla	Mission specialist
Laurel Clark	Mission specialist
William McCool	Pilot
Ilan Ramon	Payload specialist (Israeli Space Agency)

Chapter 2

Tanya Morrison

Potential Future Astronaut

"Good night, Tanya," said my mother, closing my bedroom door.

"Night, Mom," I replied as I crawled into bed and turned out the light. Immediately I looked out of my window, as I did every night. One of my favorite parts of living out in the country was that I could still look up and see so many stars overhead. Most of my friends lived in the city, and I admit, I envied them now and then. At least they didn't have a 45-minute bus ride to and from school every day. But at night, when I looked up and saw more stars than I could begin to count, I considered myself the lucky one. City lights made it impossible to see the stars. Here, they were endless.

▲ *Light pollution is when there is too much artificial light. This excess light makes it hard to see the stars.*

For years, I had wondered what it would be like to travel among the stars. My parents had gotten me a telescope for my 10th birthday, and I used it to learn everything I could about the planets and **constellations**. Every science fair project I did was on space travel. I read every science-fiction book the library had. I could quote lines from more than a dozen space travel movies. I was determined to grow up and become an astronaut. I already knew the requirements: a bachelor's degree in computer science, engineering, biological or physical science, or math; 1,000 hours of flying time in a jet plane (or three years of professional experience); and a standard **physical**. I had years to work on

Second Source

▶ Find a second source that describes the qualifications for becoming an astronaut. Compare the information there to the information in this source.

those—most astronauts were between the ages of 26 and 46, and I am only 12.

The thought of discovering new worlds, using incredibly high-tech scientific equipment, and coping with a lack of **gravity** sounded fascinating to me. I had to admit that wearing one of those cool space suits and keeping an eye out for friendly or hostile aliens

▲ *Having a strong background in engineering is helpful for astronauts and NASA scientists.*

Think About It

▶ Read the last paragraph on page 19. What is the main point? Give two reasons why you think this.

sounded even better. Up until today, I knew that becoming an astronaut was in my future. I could barely wait for that day to come.

And then the *Columbia* space shuttle blew up as it headed back toward Earth. Now I am not so sure about my future. Watching that happen on TV was horrifying. The astronauts were only minutes away from landing. "Those poor people," my mother had whispered, tears running down her face.

I knew space travel was dangerous, of course, but the risk always seemed to be outweighed by the sense of adventure and exploration. History was full of people who ventured into new lands to find treasure and other discoveries. Astronauts did the same thing, but they went beyond our planet to see what mysteries could be found in the universe. They were modern heroes, riding huge rockets into space to learn what was in the blackness surrounding Earth.

But watching the *Columbia* break apart and scatter in the sky made me question everything about space travel. Was I willing to risk my life to go into space and study what's out there? Was what any astronaut learned important enough to balance the money and danger?

▲ *NASA astronauts must be able to work in a zero gravity environment.*

▲ *The Super Soaker squirt gun was invented in 1989 by a NASA engineer.*

Thinking back on all I had learned over the years about space exploration, I knew my answer would still be yes, it was worth it. The space program needed to keep going for many reasons. One day, we might need another planet to live on, so we had to keep looking for one that allowed human survival. Also, space missions have helped develop important technology, from robotic arms used in surgery to portable vacuum cleaners for houses. Most of all, we need to keep going into space because it is natural for humans to want to explore. I know I still want to—especially if I get to find an alien in the process!

Astronaut in Training

For kids who want to one day be an astronaut, training can begin now. Physical exercises that improve your agility, coordination, balance, speed, and strength can make passing that NASA exam one day much easier. Find exercises and videos for training like an astronaut at NASA's site, www.nasa.gov/audience/foreducators/trainlikeanastronaut/activities.

Chapter 3

Rufus Connor

Illinois Student

The living room was almost silent. My father, older brother, Samuel, and I all watched as the *Columbia* space shuttle fell apart. It was awful. I had never seen anything like it. I could feel tears in my eyes.

"See, boys? THIS is exactly why we should stop throwing our money away on the space program," my father said, his voice angry and shaken. "This mission probably cost billions of tax dollars, and what do we have to show for it? We just lost seven lives for nothing." He shook his head.

▲ *In 2011, the average cost to launch a Space Shuttle mission was about $450 million.*

Analyze This

▶ How is Mr. Connor's perspective on space exploration different from Tanya's perspective? How are they similar?

Samuel glanced over at me. I shrugged. I knew Dad was too upset to argue with right now. I always thought the space program looked exciting, but after today's explosion, I wasn't so sure.

"You're right, Dad," Samuel said. "We could have used all of that money to help problems right here on good old planet Earth. Think what could have been done with those billions if we had used it for feeding the hungry, housing the homeless, or working to improve the impact of **climate change**."

I had no idea Samuel agreed with Dad. Were they right? I thought about it. I guess exploring the stars and planets is not necessary for human beings' survival. Wouldn't it be better to dedicate all of that money and time to exploring parts of *our* planet, like the oceans?

▲ *U.S. aid could help reduce extreme poverty around the world.*

"I heard in school that 95 percent of the world's oceans have never been seen by human eyes," I said. "They are almost completely unexplored. Maybe we should look there instead."

"Good idea, Rufus," Dad said. "I know that a lot of those science types point out how many high-tech items have been developed thanks to space travel, but the average person will never use any of these things."

I thought about what Mr. Tomlinson, my science teacher, had told us about what he called space spin-offs. He had described medical and exercise equipment that had helped countless people. He also talked about how space technology had led to robots that might one day fight fires or carry heavy loads in order to protect humans. Now I was confused. If the average person doesn't need or use the technology, are these space-related breakthroughs worth it?

"I read that space exploration is bad for the astronauts," I said. "Being in zero gravity can make their bones get brittle, and it can make body muscles get weaker."

That reminded me of something my best friend, Leo, had said the other day. "I heard that each time any type of mission goes up, debris gets left behind," Leo had said. "NASA stated that hundreds of thousands of man-made objects are in **orbit**."

A Curious Species

Reporter Stuart Atkinson wrote, "Some say we should stop exploring space, that the cost in human lives is too great. But *Columbia*'s crew would not have wanted that. We are a curious species, always wanting to know what is over the next hill, around the next corner, on the next island. And we have been that way for thousands of years."

Second Source

▶ Find a second source that describes the different items that have been invented due to space travel. Compare the information there to the perspectives of Mr. Connor and Rufus. How are they different? How are they similar?

"Like what?" I had asked him.

"Everything from pieces of spacecraft and satellites that break off to pieces of paint or batteries," Leo replied.

I told Dad about this. "Space trash?" he asked with a chuckle. "That's a new one to me!"

We spent the rest of the evening watching the news updates. Seeing the sadness on everyone's faces was hard. My dad, brother, and I kept discussing the explosion up until bedtime. When I finally crawled under the covers, I was still confused. The idea of going to space was an exciting one, but I realized, perhaps for the first time, that it was also a pretty **controversial** one.

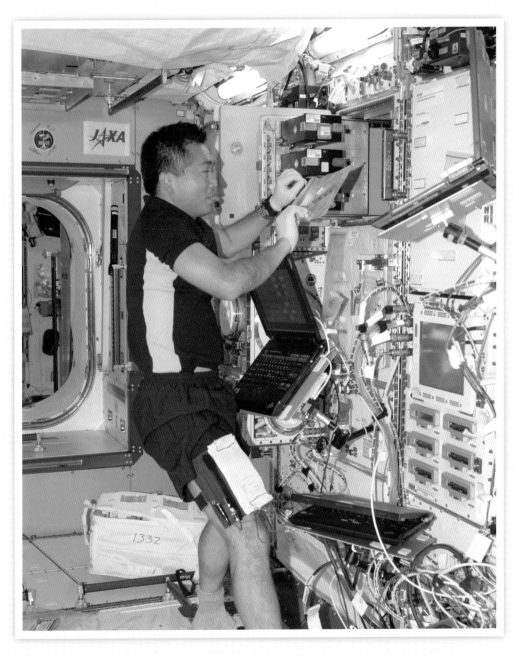

▲ *NASA's mission statement is "to pioneer the future in space exploration, scientific discovery and aeronautics research."*

Look, Look Again

Look closely at this photo of a memorial to fallen astronauts and use it to answer the questions below:

1. How might someone in the media report on this image?

2. What would a future astronaut think about this? How might their family feel about this image?

3. What would a family concerned about government spending think about this image? How might that be different from what a future astronaut would think?

Glossary

climate change (KLYE-mit CHAYNJ) a long-term change in Earth's climate (weather and temperature)

constellations (kahn-stuh-LAY-shuhnz) groups of stars

controversial (kahn-truh-VUR-shuhl) subject to debate or argument

gravity (GRAV-ih-tee) the force of attraction by which bodies tend to fall toward the center of the earth

launch (LAWNCH) to send forth or release a vehicle

liftoff (LIFT-awf) the action of an aircraft to become airborne

NASA (NAH-suh) the National Aeronautics and Space Administration

orbit (OR-bit) the curved path around a celestial body

payload (PAY-lohd) the load carried by a spacecraft consisting of things necessary to the purpose of the flight

physical (FIZ-ih-kuhl) a thorough or complete medical test

reentry (ree-EN-tree) the return from outer space into Earth's atmosphere

Learn More

Further Reading

Cole, Michael. *The* Columbia *Space Shuttle Disaster: From First Liftoff to Tragic Final Flight.* Berkeley Heights, NJ: Enslow Publishers, 2003.

Feldman, Heather. Columbia: *The First Space Shuttle.* New York: Rosen Publishing, 2006.

Krumm, Brian. *Shuttle in the Sky: The* Columbia *Disaster.* North Mankato, MN: Capstone Publishing, 2016.

Schafer, Christopher. *The Space Shuttle* Columbia *Explosion.* Minneapolis: ABDO Publishing, 2004.

Web Sites

DK Find Out!—The Space Shuttle
www.dkfindout.com/us/space/space-shuttle

History Channel—*Columbia* Disaster
www.history.com/topics/columbia-disaster

Kids Astronomy.com—Space Shuttle
www.kidsastronomy.com/space_shuttle.htm

Index

About the Author

Tamra Orr remembers seeing the *Columbia* explosion on television. She is the author of hundreds of books for readers of all ages. She lives in the Pacific Northwest with her family and spends all of her free time writing letters, reading books, and going camping. She graduated from Ball State University with a degree in English and education, and believes she has the best job in the world. It gives her the chance to keep learning all about the world and the people in it.